O9-ABE-959

Disasters for All Time

THE DEEPWATER HORIZON OIL SPILL

Valerie Bodden

CREATIVE EDUCATION • CREATIVE PAPERBACKS

Published by Creative Education
and Creative Paperbacks
P.O. Box 227, Mankato, Minnesota 56002

Creative Education and Creative Paperbacks
are imprints of The Creative Company
www.thecreativecompany.us

Design and production by Joe Kahnke
Art direction by Rita Marshall
Printed in China

Photographs by Alamy (Ted Horowitz, Barry Iverson, ZUMA Press, Inc.), CineRoxy, Creative Commons
Wikimedia (Ensign Jason Radcliffe/U.S. Coast Guard, Petty Officer 3rd Class Barry Bena/U.S. Coast Guard,
Petty Officer 3rd Class Patrick Kelley/DVIDS, Pete Souza/The Obama-Biden Transition Project, U.S. Coast
Guard), DVIDS (Petty Officer 3rd Class Patrick Kelley), Flickr (Roy Vest), Getty Images (Bloomberg, Win
McNamee/Getty Images News, Vernon Merritt III/The LIFE Picture Collection, Joe Raedle/Getty Images
News), iStockphoto (baona, Dazman, HeliRy, landbysea, nielubieklonu), Newscom (LEE CELANO/REUTERS,
Bob Hallinen/MCT), Reuters (REUTERS/Hans Deryk), Shutterstock (Hindrik Johannes de Groot, PixOne,
Nisalwa Raden-Ahmad, Ingvar Tjostheim, vectorEps), Steadfast TV, U.S. Department of Energy (Energy
Department Video)

Image on p. 45 © 2016 Jason Kimes, courtesy of the artist.

Library of Congress Cataloging-in-Publication Data
Names: Bodden, Valerie, author. Title: The *Deepwater Horizon* oil spill / by Valerie Bodden.
Series: Disasters for all time. Includes index.

Summary: A historical account—including eyewitness quotes—of the devastating 2010 explosion on the
Deepwater Horizon oil rig and the resulting oil spill's harmful environmental impact, ending with how the
disaster's victims are memorialized today.

Identifiers: LCCN 2017051378 / ISBN 978-1-64026-003-0 (hardcover)
/ ISBN 978-1-62832-548-5 (pbk) / ISBN 978-1-64000-022-3 (eBook)

Subjects: LCSH: 1. BP Deepwater Horizon Explosion and Oil Spill, 2010—Juvenile literature.
2. Oil spills—Mexico, Gulf of—Juvenile literature.

Classification: LCC TD427.P4 B595 2018 / DDC 363.11/9622338190916364—dc23

CCSS: RI.3.1-8; RI.4.1-5, 7; RI.5.1-3, 8; RI.6.1-2, 4, 7; RH.6-8.3-8

First Edition HC 9 8 7 6 5 4 3 2 1
First Edition PBK 9 8 7 6 5 4 3 2 1

CONTENTS

4.20.

The sun had already set on April 20, 2010. But crew members aboard *Deepwater Horizon* were still hard at work. This huge oil rig was located in the Gulf of Mexico. It was stationed 41 miles (66 km) from the Louisiana shore. There it floated in 5,000 feet (1,524 m) of water. The rig's crew had spent the past two and a half months drilling. They had finally reached their target: a deposit of oil deep beneath the seafloor. Now the crew had to cap the well

At first, everything seemed to go according to plan. But at 9:40 P.M., drilling fluids shot out of the drill pipe. They showered the rig's deck. The hiss of natural gas followed the fluids. The crew tried to close off the pipe. But it was too late. An explosion rocked the rig. Flames shot from the derrick. The well had blown out.

DRILLING DEEPER

People started using oil as a fuel in the 1820s. At first, it was collected from spots where it seeped to the surface of the ground. The first oil well was dug in Pennsylvania in 1859. It bored only 69 feet (21 m) into the ground. The well pumped **crude oil** from **porous** rock layers below. The crude oil could then be made into kerosene, gasoline, and other fuels.

Over time, oil became an important fuel source. Oil rigs were built across the United States and around the world. By the 1890s, oil companies were setting up rigs in shallow ocean waters along shorelines.

Then rigs were built farther from shore. The first offshore rig was built in the Gulf of Mexico in 1938. That rig was more than a mile (1.6 km) from shore. It stood in 14 feet (4.3 m) of water. Offshore rigs brought new

Onshore drilling accounts for about 70 percent of worldwide oil production.

1.28.1969
Santa Barbara, CA, oil spill

challenges and dangers. They had to be relatively small. Yet they still had to hold all the needed equipment and crew. They had to withstand the Gulf's frequent hurricanes. And they didn't have access to immediate help if something went wrong. One early offshore rig crew member later said, "Nobody really knew what they were doing at that time."

Over the years, offshore drilling rigs became larger and more advanced. They also moved to deeper ocean waters. In 1969, a rig located six miles (9.7 km) from the California shore blew out. The rig stood in 188 feet (57.3 m) of water. Nearly 100,000 barrels of oil gushed into the sea. Each barrel holds 42 gallons (159 l). So 4.2 million gallons (15.9 million l) of oil flowed into the sea. As a result of the spill, the U.S. recognized its first **Earth Day** in 1970. In 1981, Congress banned offshore drilling along more than 80 percent of America's coastlines.

A blowout in 1969 near California polluted 800 square miles (2,072 sq km) of ocean and shoreline.

Offshore Drilling Zones in the U.S.

(2008–12)

drilling prohibited

drilling permitted

Limited drilling was still allowed in the western Gulf of Mexico. There, oil companies drilled in deeper and deeper water. Any well in water deeper than 1,000 feet (305 m) is considered a deep-water well. Many wells are even deeper. By 2008, near-ly 300 wells in waters more than 5,000 feet (1,524 m) deep dotted the Gulf.

In March 2010, president Barack Obama announced that more U.S. waters would be opened to offshore drilling. Many of these waters were located along the East Coast

"In the short term, as we transition to cleaner energy sources, we've still got to make some tough decisions about opening new offshore areas for oil and gas development…. The bottom line is this: Given our energy needs, … we are going to need to harness traditional sources of fuel, even as we ramp up production of new sources of renewable, homegrown energy."

– President Barack Obama, March 31, 2010

and in the Gulf. Others were off the coast of Alaska. The president said, "Oil rigs today generally don't cause spills. They are technologically very advanced."

The rigs were advanced in terms of drilling abilities and equipment. But safety technology remained limited. Oil companies had not invested enough money into preparing for a spill. They had not worked to develop new spill cleanup measures. Government safety regulations were not updated for deep-water drilling. And gov-

ernment inspectors sometimes ignored safety violations aboard rigs. They granted drilling permits without fully reviewing oil companies' spill safety plans.

By 2010, about 4,000 wells were actively pumping oil in the Gulf of Mexico. The region provided about one-third of the oil produced in America. New oil reserves continued to be discovered beneath its waters. Most Gulf oil wells were located in 1,000 feet (305 m) or less of water. But some of

the newest oil discoveries were thousands of feet below the seafloor in deep water. Rigs extracting oil from this depth faced extra dangers. The oil reserves were under enormous **pressure** from the weight of the water and seabed above. When a well was cut into these reserves, the pressure had to be controlled. Otherwise, oil and gas could shoot to the surface. Despite such dangers, rigs kept drilling. There was still more oil to be found.

EXXON VALDEZ

In 1989, people around the country watched their TVs in horror. They saw images of wild-life covered in oil from *Exxon Valdez*. The ship had run aground in Alaska. It spilled nearly 11 million gallons (41.6 million l) of oil. Afterward, new laws and regulations were enacted. Most had to do with preventing spills from oil tankers. They did not address safety aboard offshore rigs.

LARGEST OIL SPILLS

1991 Gulf War oil spills
250+ million gallons (946+ million l)

2010 Deepwater Horizon
210 million gallons (795 million l)

1979 Ixtoc 1 well
140 million gallons (530 million l)

1992 Fergana Valley oil spill
88 million gallons (333 million l)

1983 Nowruz oil field
80 million gallons (303 million l)

(1) (2) (3) (4) (5)

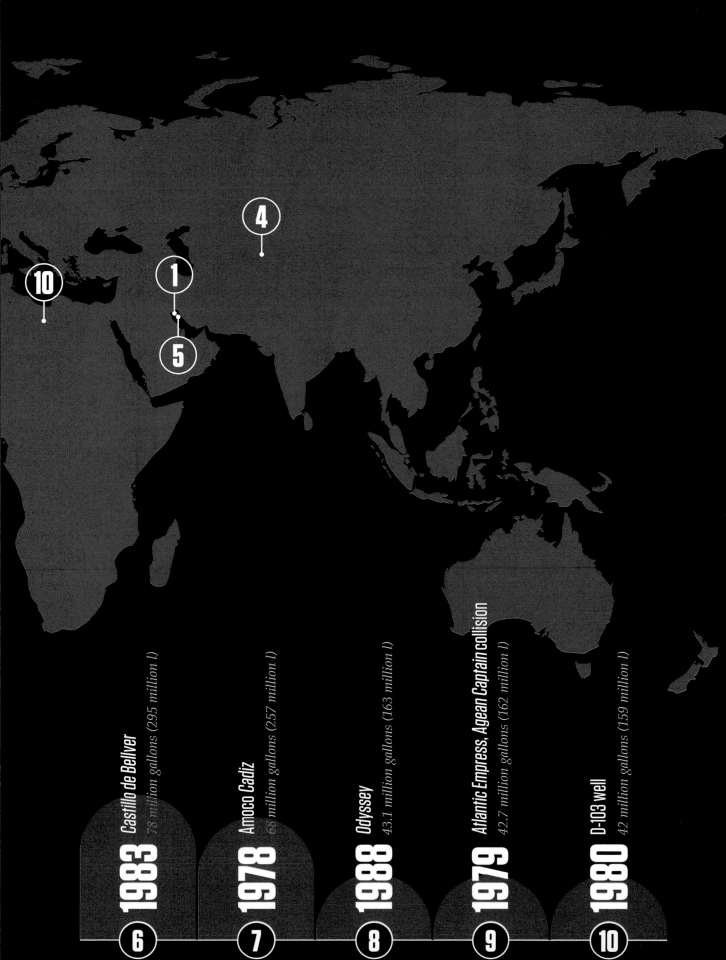

1983 Castillo de Bellver
78 million gallons (295 million l)

1978 Amoco Cadiz
68 million gallons (257 million l)

1988 Odyssey
43.1 million gallons (163 million l)

1979 Atlantic Empress, Agean Captain collision
42.7 million gallons (162 million l)

1980 D-103 well
42 million gallons (159 million l)

6 7 8 9 10

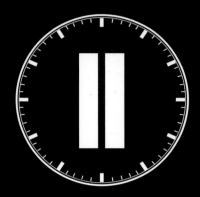

DIGGING THE MACONDO WELL

To drill in offshore waters, a company needs a **lease** from the U.S. government. Dozens of oil companies hold leases to drilling rights in Gulf waters. Among the largest is BP. In March 2008, BP purchased drilling rights for a location 41 miles (66 km) southeast of Louisiana. It named the spot Macondo. The water there was 5,000 feet (1,524 m) deep. BP thought oil might be found another 13,000 feet (3,962 m) beneath the seafloor.

Like many oil companies, BP did not have its own drilling rigs. Instead, the company leased a rig and crew from Swiss-based Transocean. The rig originally chosen to drill the site was the *Marianas*. Drilling began in October 2009. But the *Marianas* was damaged by a hurricane in November. It had to be towed to shore for repairs.

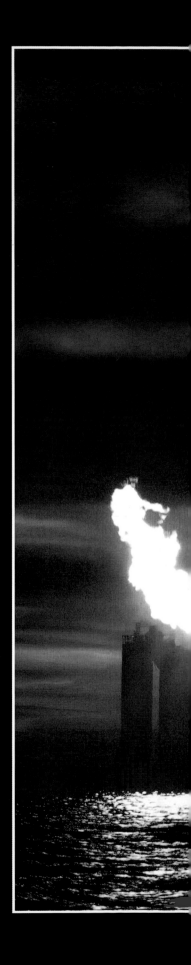

When oil is extracted from a well, natural gas is usually present; the gas is burned off in a process known as flaring.

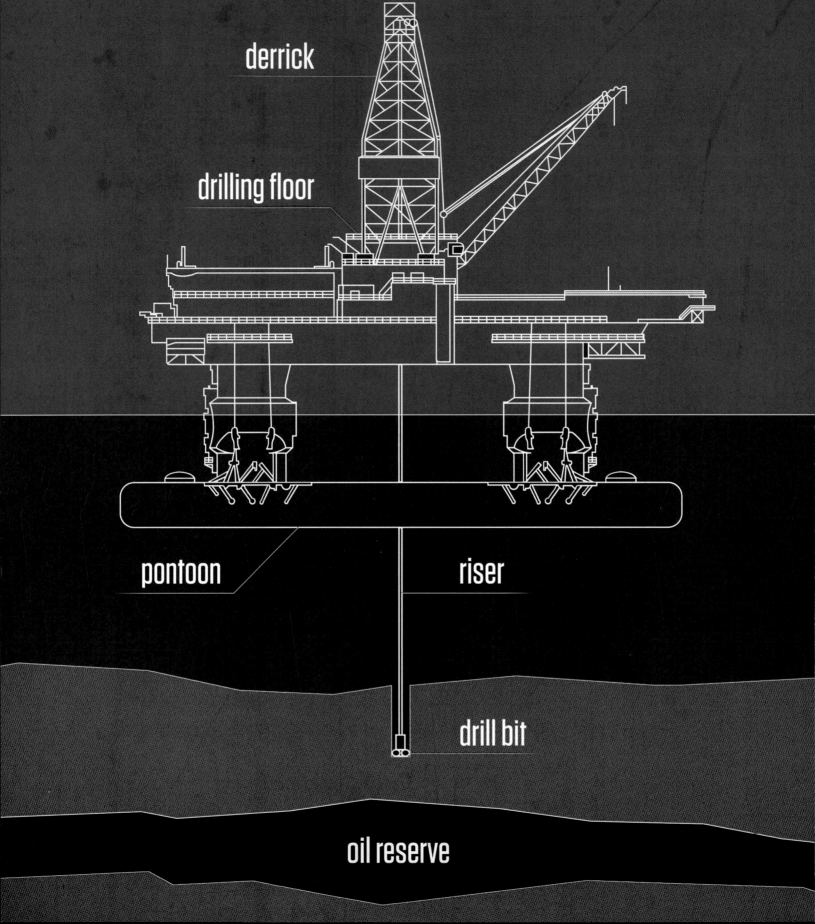

derrick

drilling floor

pontoon

riser

drill bit

oil reserve

On January 31, 2010, Transocean sent a new rig. It was called *Deepwater Horizon*. The rig floated on two giant **pontoons**. A dynamic positioning system used data from **satellites** to keep the rig centered above the location of the well.

Four thick columns rose from the pontoons. They supported the rig's four decks.

The highest deck was the drill floor. Drilling operations were controlled from here. An oil derrick rose 244 feet (74.4 m) above this deck. Beneath the drill floor was the main deck. It contained the rig's main controls. The lower two decks held offices and crew quarters.

Deepwater Horizon housed a crew of

24/7 RIG

The crew kept *Deepwater Horizon* operating 24 hours a day. Each crew member worked a 12-hour night or day shift. Then he or she had 12 hours off. During downtime, the crew could visit the rig's movie theater or gym. Crew members worked for three weeks straight. Then they had three weeks off. Helicopters flew them back and forth between the rig and shore. Ships brought needed supplies.

126. About 80 worked for Transocean. Six worked for BP. Two of the BP employees directed drilling operations. Another 40 crew members worked for other companies **contracted** by BP.

On February 6, 2010, *Deepwater Horizon* began drilling. As the drill pushed through the rock, a heavy liquid called drilling fluid, or mud, was sent through the well. The fluid put downward pressure on the well. This kept the upward pressure of the oil and gas from pushing into the drill pipe. It also brought rock shavings back to the surface. As the well grew deeper, the crew lowered metal casings into it. These lined the well. They were cemented into place.

Many companies use remotely operated vehicles fitted with cameras to inspect underwater equipment such as blowout preventers.

Together, the casings, drilling mud, and cement kept oil and gas from coming up the well. If something went wrong, the crew could close the blowout preventer. This was a 50-foot-high (15.2 m) stack of **valves**. It sat on top of the well at the seafloor. It connected the well to the riser—the long pipe that led from the rig to the wellhead. In an emergency, the valves of the blowout preventer could be closed. This would trap gas and oil in the well so that they couldn't flow up the riser and onto the rig.

THE DEEPWATER HORIZON OIL SPILL

RIG PROBLEMS

Deepwater Horizon had been state-of-the-art when it was built for $350 million in 2001. But by 2010, some of its equipment was out-of-date. The computers that monitored drilling operations sometimes froze. Some crew members worried about safety violations aboard the rig. But only hours before the blowout, BP officials presented the crew with a safety award. They had gone seven years without a major injury.

Depending on rig size, as few as a dozen or as many as 200 crew members may live and work on offshore platforms.

By April 9, the Macondo well was 54 days behind schedule. It was $58 million over budget.

As drilling at Macondo continued, the crew ran into problems. In early April, they experienced "lost returns." This meant that none of the drilling mud pumped into the well came back up. Instead, it seeped into the rock sides of the well. If that continued, the crew would not be able to maintain the correct pressure in the well. Oil and gas might come spouting to the surface. The crew fixed the problem by pouring a thick liquid into the well. It coated the well walls. This kept more drilling fluid from seeping into the rock.

Finally, on April 9, the crew reached their target depth: 18,360 feet (5,596 m) below the sea's surface. The well was now 54 days behind schedule. It was $58 million over budget. And it cost BP $1 million for each extra day *Deepwater Horizon* remained at Macondo. The crew needed to finish the job.

RIG ON FIRE

Deepwater Horizon's job had been to drill the well. Another smaller rig would come to extract the oil. Before *Deepwater Horizon* could leave, though, the well had to be cemented shut. BP contracted with the company Halliburton for the cementing job.

Around 7:30 P.M. on April 19, cement began flowing into the well. The process took five hours. After the cement hardened, it was supposed to be tested. The test would create a model of the cement job. It would identify any holes or openings in the cement. The test was supposed to be carried out by another contractor, Schlumberger. A team from Schlumberger was already on the rig. But BP officials decided they didn't need the test. They sent the Schlumberger crew home.

Then the crew members performed their own tests. These were different from the ones Schlumberger would

A large rig is like a floating city and may provide a restaurant, movie theater, gym, and laundry services for personnel.

UNSTABLE CEMENT

Cement for deep-water wells has to withstand extreme temperatures and pressures. Crew members from Halliburton created a special mixture for the Macondo well. Before using it, they sent it to a lab for testing. The results showed that the cement might become unstable under the conditions present in the well. But neither Halliburton nor BP raised concerns about using it.

have used. The crew began with a positive pressure test. For this test, they increased the pressure on the well. If the pressure remained steady, it meant nothing was leaking out of the well. The positive pressure test was successful.

Next, the crew performed a negative pressure test. For this test, they removed pressure from the well. They wanted to get the pressure down to zero in two pipes—the drill line and the kill line. This would mean that no oil or gas was leaking into the

well from below. It would show that the cement was holding.

The crew began the negative pressure test at 3:00 P.M. on April 20. For the next several hours, they tried to get the pressure down to zero. The pressure in the kill line reached zero. But pressure in the drill line kept creeping back up. The crew performed the test several times. Each time, they got the same results. Even so, by 8:00 P.M., they decided that zero pressure in one line was enough. They declared the test a success.

Roughly an hour after the crew declared the negative stress test a success, they noticed the pressure increasing in the well.

The next step was to insert another cement plug closer to the top of the well. But first, the crew had to replace the drilling mud in the well with lighter-weight seawater. At 8:02 P.M., they began pumping heavy drilling fluids out of the well. Pressure on the well decreased as they pumped seawater into the well. But around 9:00 P.M., pressure slowly began to increase. This may have signaled that oil or gas had entered the well. But the crew kept pumping. Finally, around 9:30, they turned the pumps off. Even then, the pressure continued to rise.

The crew looked for a cause. Before they could find one, drilling fluids shot out of the derrick and rained down onto the rig floor. The crew realized there had been a blowout. They tried to close the valves on the blowout preventer. But gas and oil continued to rush up from the well.

At 9:49 P.M., gas burst onto the rig, causing an explosion. More explosions followed. Fires broke

Two days after the explosions, Deepwater Horizon capsized and sank beneath the Gulf waters.

"I made it to the doorway of the … office when a tremendous explosion occurred. It blew me probably 20 feet (6.1 m)…. The lights went out…. I could hear everything deathly calm…. I had a lot of debris on top of me. I tried two different times to get up…. The third time … I pulled [my trapped leg] as hard as I could, and it came free."

– Randy Ezell, Deepwater Horizon *crew member*

out everywhere. The crew tried to activate the rig's emergency disconnect system (EDS). This was supposed to disconnect the rig from the wellhead. But the EDS didn't respond. There was no way to stop the flow of gas and oil.

Crew members raced for the rig's lifeboats. In their panic, they pushed off before everyone was aboard. Those stranded on the fiery rig jumped. It was a 10-story fall to the water. A supply ship called *Bankston* was near the rig. Its crew saw the explosion. They pulled the people who had jumped out of the water. Those in the lifeboats boarded the *Bankston*, too. Eleven people on *Deepwater Horizon* had died. Another 17 were injured. From aboard the *Bankston*, the survivors watched their rig burn.

Coast Guard rescuers who rushed to the scene could see the blaze from 90 miles (145 km) away.

The Macondo oil spill caused pollution in both the water and the air, as the fire emitted black soot and fumes.

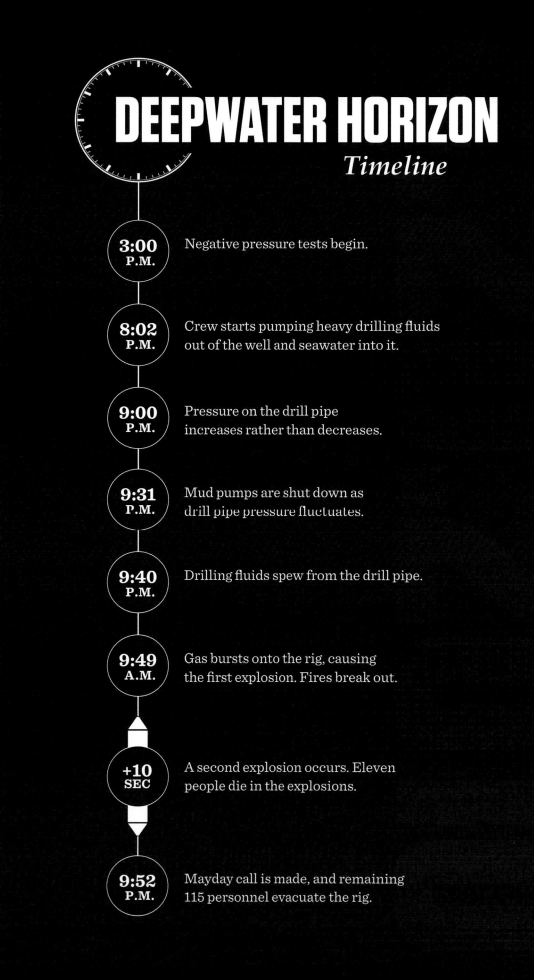

DEEPWATER HORIZON
Timeline

3:00 P.M. — Negative pressure tests begin.

8:02 P.M. — Crew starts pumping heavy drilling fluids out of the well and seawater into it.

9:00 P.M. — Pressure on the drill pipe increases rather than decreases.

9:31 P.M. — Mud pumps are shut down as drill pipe pressure fluctuates.

9:40 P.M. — Drilling fluids spew from the drill pipe.

9:49 A.M. — Gas bursts onto the rig, causing the first explosion. Fires break out.

+10 SEC — A second explosion occurs. Eleven people die in the explosions.

9:52 P.M. — Mayday call is made, and remaining 115 personnel evacuate the rig.

IV

LASTING EFFECTS

Deepwater Horizon burned for two days. On April 22—
Earth Day—the rig sank. The next day, remote cameras
showed oil leaking from the riser pipe. The pipe had
broken off when the rig sank. The first official reports
from BP said the pipe was leaking 1,000 barrels a day.
But scientists soon estimated the flow to be closer to
50,000 barrels a day.

Working with the Coast Guard, BP tried to clean
up the oil. Fishermen were hired to place containment
booms in the Gulf. Booms are huge inflatable floats.
They are made of a material that can absorb oil. The
booms were placed along shorelines. They were supposed to block oil from reaching shore. But waves
washed oily water over the tops of the booms.

BP also applied dispersants to the oil. These are
chemicals that help break down oil. Then the oil can't

Researchers concluded that at least eight different safety measures that should have been in place on Deepwater Horizon failed.

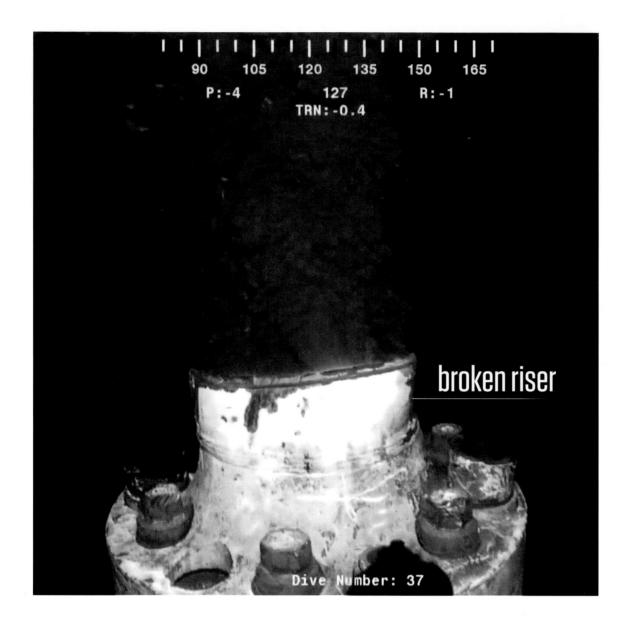

broken riser

Dive Number: 37

coat wildlife. But many people worried that the dispersants might be harmful to wildlife and to people. Many of the fishermen hired to spread the chemicals became ill.

BP also worked to stop the flow of oil. By the end of May, the company had made several failed attempts. In early June, BP fit a loose cap on the end of the riser pipe. A pipe allowed boats at the surface to collect a fraction of the oil spilling from the well. But most of the oil continued to spew into the sea.

In July, a new, tighter-fitting cap was attached to the pipe. This cap included a series of seals. On July 15, the seals on the cap were successfully closed. The flow of oil finally stopped. In September, the well was cemented shut.

Despite various cleanup attempts, roughly 75 percent of the oil spilled remained in the water.

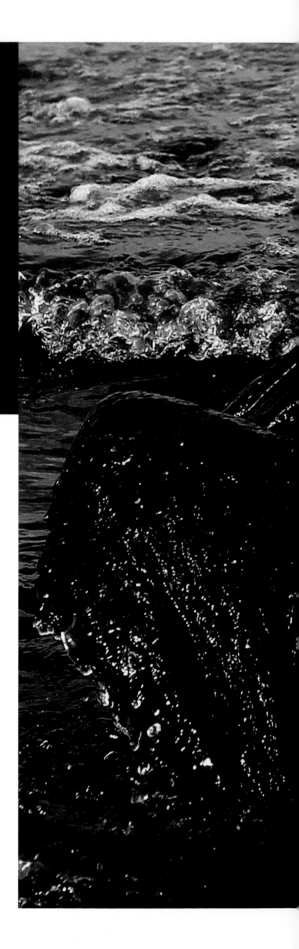

Early reports suggested the pipe was leaking 1,000 barrels of oil per day. But scientists soon estimated the flow to be closer to 50,000 barrels each day.

By then, nearly 5 million barrels of oil had leaked into the Gulf. The spill was the largest ever to occur in a body of water. Much of the oil stayed in deep water. But oil also washed up on nearly 1,100 miles (1,770 km) of coast. Beaches from Florida to Texas were oiled. Dead birds, turtles, and dolphins washed up along shorelines.

President Obama created the National Commission on the BP *Deepwater Horizon* Oil Spill and Offshore Drilling. The commission's job was to investigate the disaster. It released its final report in January 2011. The report concluded that BP management had failed to properly assess the risks. It called for changes in oil industry regulations. It also urged the development of new techniques for responding to deep-water oil spills.

During the first year after the disaster, an estimated 6,000 birds—including gulls, gannets, and pelicans—were found dead.

"[Hurricane] Katrina [in 2005] destroyed us—but it didn't kill us. A hurricane takes everything, but you know you're gonna come back. You know you're gonna have the seafood, sport fishing…. But the oil … could take all this away from us. What do you do then?… Eventually, this is gonna go away. Whether it's going to take everybody with it, that I don't know."

Frank Campo, owner of a Louisiana fishing station

Scientists still do not know the long-term effects the oil spill will have on the ecosystem of Louisiana's swamps and marshes.

Following the blowout, BP faced an estimated $62 billion in fees. These included fines, cleanup costs, and **settlements**. At least $15 billion was set aside to help with efforts to restore the natural environment in the Gulf. By 2015, many animals seemed to be recovering from the spill. But scientists warned it could take years to learn the full effects on wildlife.

After the disaster, BP's Macondo site was closed to drilling. But in 2015, oil company LLOG was allowed to begin drilling three miles (4.8 km) from Macondo. LLOG vowed to keep "the memory of what happened [aboard the *Deepwater Horizon*] fresh" as they drilled. They said it inspired them to put safety first.

Others kept the memory of the disaster

WAKE-UP CALL

People urged the government to see the *Deepwater Horizon* disaster as a wake-up call. They wanted more money invested in clean energy sources. Such sources include wind, water, and solar power. The National Commission said that the spill did not mean the country had to abandon deep-water drilling. But it encouraged Americans to "consider the broader context of the nation's patterns of energy production and use, now and in the future."

alive through a memorial installed in New Orleans in 2016. Titled *Eleven*, the memorial consists of 11 life-size sculptures to represent those killed in the disaster. The sculptures were made of small steel disks. The steel reflected life aboard the oil rig.

Today, the spot where *Deepwater Horizon* once floated is open ocean. No signs of the rig or the lives lost there remain. Yet the impact of the rig's violent end continues to be felt.

GLOSSARY

contracted paid to provide a specific service

crude oil oil in its natural form, as from an oil well

derrick the structure that raises and lowers the drilling pipe in an oil well

Earth Day an annual celebration (held each April 22) to promote environmental issues

lease an agreement to use a property or structure for a certain amount of time in return for a fee

pontoons large cylinders that float and support a boat, seaplane, or floating drilling rig

porous filled with tiny holes that allow liquids to pass through

pressure force exerted by pressing on an object or substance

satellites artificial objects that orbit a planet or moon and collect information to send back to Earth

settlements agreements or payments made by one person or company to another to settle a dispute or lawsuit

valves devices that open or close to allow or block the flow of fluids or gases

READ MORE

Stone, Adam. *The Deepwater Horizon Oil Spill.* Minneapolis: Bellwether Media, 2014.

Wang, Andrea. *The Science of an Oil Spill.* Ann Arbor, Mich.: Cherry Lake, 2015.

WEBSITES

Smithsonian Ocean Portal: Gulf of Mexico Oil Spill Interactive
http://ocean.si.edu/gulf-mexico-oil-spill-interactive

Learn more about the impact of the oil spill and cleanup efforts in the Gulf of Mexico.

National Geographic: Oil Spills
https://www.nationalgeographic.org/education/oil-spills/

Check out information and activities about oil spills.

Note: Every effort has been made to ensure that any websites listed above were active at the time of publication. However, because of the nature of the Internet, it is impossible to guarantee that these sites will remain active indefinitely or that their contents will not be altered.

INDEX